I0464664

Legal Matrix

of

Ukraine

Business Entity

ALLA DOMBROVSKA

Copyright © 2015 Alla Dombrovska

All rights reserved.

ISBN-13: 978-1514307748
ISBN-10: 151430774X

CONTENTS

PREFACE

Today, after almost twenty four years of the Ukrainian independence, the building of a modern legal system is still one of the top priorities of the state. The notion that a legal system and a legal tradition is totally absent, a sort of *tabula rasa*, is ruined by the fact that Ukraine always has had an established legal system based on the Continental Law. Thus, the core of Ukrainian Civil Law became *das Bürgerliches Gesetzbuch (BGB)*, the German Civil Code. Despite the socialistic model of economy, the principal areas of law, such as the law of contracts, civil law obligations, liabilities, torts, as well as applicability of choice of the law and international arbitration to international business transactions, were based on European tradition.

The change of economy model had a significant impact on the legislation in general and on the business law in particular. Since 1991, the year of gaining the independence by Ukraine, a number of normative acts regulating the economic relationships were adopted. There were codified acts like the Civil Code, the Economic Code, the Tax Code, and a series of laws such as "On State Registration of Legal Entities and Individual Entrepreneurs", "On Business Associations", "On Joint Stock Companies", "On Renewal of the Debtor's Solvency or Declaring Its Bankruptcy" etc. Some of the laws adopted in the early 1990s have already been abolished ("On ownership", "On Entrepreneurship", "On Enterprises") and replaced with others.

Such significant bulk of legislation related to business regulation made the functioning of various legal forms of enterprises and a number of different types of economic activity possible. Undoubtedly, the legal system currently existing in Ukraine, in spite of its flaws and complications, does provide a certain legal basis for running business and protecting the legitimate interests of the parties involved.

What is a business activity under the provisions of legislation acts? What are the legal forms of business entities, which may conduct their activity? What are the rules of performing entrepreneurship?

"Legal Matrix of Ukraine. Business Entity" will help to answer these and many other questions arising in concern with ascertaining rights and duties of persons taking part in business transactions as well as determining the scope of influence of government and local authorities on business activity in Ukraine.

1 NOTION OF BUSINESS ACTIVITY IN UKRAINE

First of all, let's figure out some facts about business activity, like what an entrepreneurship is and what the diverse legal forms of business entities are. You will find out who is eligible to perform business activity and what its basic principles are. Besides, you will have an answer to a question how and why business entities are divided into small, micro, large and medium and what fraud in performing business activity is.

Upon the provisions of the Economic Code of Ukraine the **economic activity** is the activity of **business entities** in the area of social production that embodies manufacturing and sale of products, execution of works or providing services. The results of such activity are products, works or services that can be valued, and have the determined price.

The economic activity is considered **entrepreneurship** if it has a purpose of generating profit, besides achieving economic and social results. However, if economic activity is carried out without purpose of generating profit it is a **non-profit economic activity**[1].

Entrepreneurship is defined as an independent, initiative, systematic, own-risk economic activity that is carried out by business entities with the purpose of achieving economic and social results, and generating profit[2]. Business entities that conduct it are deemed entrepreneurs.

It is presumed that entrepreneurs have the right to perform any entrepreneurial activity that is not banned by the law independently and without any limitations. Peculiarities of performing certain types of entrepreneurship are outlined by legislative acts of Ukraine. The list of types of

---

[1] The Economic Code of Ukraine, Article 3, Part II, III
[2] The Economic Code of Ukraine, Article 42

business activity subject to licensing, as well as the list of activities, wherein entrepreneurship is banned must be established exclusively by the law. Ukrainian state authorities and local governments as well as their officials are not eligible to carry out entrepreneurial activity.

The entire body of principles makes a framework of a business activity. Thus, the entrepreneurship is conducted on the basis of:

(a)   free choice by the entrepreneur of a type of business activity;
(b)   independent development by the entrepreneur of his/her/its activity program, selection of suppliers and consumers of products manufactured, the use of material, technical, financial and other resources, which are not limited by the law, fixing of prices of products and services;
(c)   free employment of personnel by the entrepreneur;
(d)   commercial calculation and own commercial risk;
(e)   free disposal of retained profit, left after payment of taxes, fees and other payments;
(f)   independent performing of foreign economic activity by the entrepreneur;
(g)   use of a share of foreign currency income at the entrepreneur's own discretion[3].

Entrepreneurship may be conducted by business entities of any legal form, envisaged by the Ukrainian legislation, at the entrepreneur's choice.

According to the Economic Code of Ukraine **business entities** related to the practicing of economic activity are divided into **individual entrepreneurs** and **economic organizations**[4].

Besides, depending on the number of employees and revenue of any activities for the year, business entities may belong to small business (including microbusiness), medium-size and large business entities that are taken into account for the purpose of taxing:

1/ the **microbusiness entities** are:

individual entrepreneurs and economic organizations whose average number of employees during the reporting period (calendar year) does not exceed 10 persons and annual income from any activity does not exceed the equivalent of 2 million euros;

2/ the **small business entities** are:

individual entrepreneurs and economic organizations whose average

---

[3] The Economic Code of Ukraine, Article 44
[4] The Economic Code of Ukraine, Article 55, part II

number of employees during the reporting period (calendar year) does not exceed 50 persons and annual income from any activity does not exceed the equivalent of 10 million euros;

3/ **large business entities** are economic organizations – business entities of any legal form and form of property whose average number of employees during the reporting period (calendar year) exceeds 250 persons and annual income from any activity exceeds the equivalent of 50 million euros;

4/ the rest business entities are the **medium-size**.

Business entities have a status of a legal entity and operate on the basis of the right of **ownership**, the right of **economic supervision**[5], and the right of **operational management**[6].

The right of economic supervision and the right of operational management are used in cases when business entities are not eligible to have property on the right of ownership, e.g. state-owned and municipal enterprises.

Business entities have right to establish **branches**, **representative offices** and other **separate divisions**. The law does not require the state registration of separate divisions as legal entities. At the same time the information about separate divisions of business entities must be included to the **Unified State Register**.

Representative offices, branches of foreign companies must be accredited on the territory of Ukraine in the manner prescribed by the law.

The Economic Code introduces the concept of **fictitious business activity**[7]. There are signs of fraudulence, which give the grounds for appeal to the court about the termination of the legal entity or the termination of activity

---

[5] **Economic supervision** – a property right of business entity that possesses, uses and disposes of the property assigned to it by the owner (authorized body), with the restriction of legal powers with regard to certain types of property upon consent of the owner in cases envisaged by the Economic Code of Ukraine and other laws.

[6] **Operational management** - a property right of a business entity that possesses, uses and disposes of the property assigned to a relevant owner (authorized body) to exercise non-profit economic activity within the limits provided by the Economic Code of Ukraine and other laws, as well as by the property owner (authorized body).

[7] The Economic Code of Ukraine, Article 55[1]

of individual entrepreneurs, including recognition of registration documents void:

I.   The entity is registered (reregistered) with invalid (lost) and forged documents.

II.   The entity is not registered while the registration duty is provided by the law.

III.   The entity is registered (re-registered) in the bodies of state registration with subsequent transfer of the rights of ownership or management to a dummy (non-existent), deceased, missing persons or to such persons who had no intention to carry out financial and economic activity.

IV.   The entity is registered (re-registered) and carries out financial and economic activity without the consent of its founders and managers appointed in a legal way.

A business entity must be subject to the state registration as a legal entity or an individual entrepreneur. A business entity may have a seal. Any permissive documents for making a seal are not required[8].

---

[8] The Economic Code of Ukraine, Article 58[1]

2 BUSINESS ENTITIES. BASIC PROVISIONS

An individual may be involved in business activity directly as an entrepreneur or through a private enterprise set up by the individual with or without the employed labor, independently or jointly with other persons.

An individual conducts management of the private enterprise directly by him/her or by supervisor hired on the contractual basis. In the case of providing business activity jointly with other natural persons or legal entities, the individual has rights and obligations of a founder and/or partner of a company, a member of cooperative, etc., or rights and obligations stipulated by the contract made with his/her participation on joint activity without establishing a legal entity.

Here you will find out how to become an individual entrepreneur and what legal conditions of creating legal entities are.

I. Individual entrepreneurs

The Economic Code names three categories of individuals that may be considered **individual entrepreneurs**. These are citizens of Ukraine, foreigners, and stateless persons that conduct business activity and are registered as **entrepreneurs**.

A natural person with full legal capability has the right to provide business activity. Generally the full legal capability arises at the age of 18 (full age).

In case of marriage of a natural person under full age, he/she acquires a full legal capability since the moment of his/her marriage registration.

In the event of marriage termination prior to the natural person attains the acquired full legal capability the last one shall be maintained[9].

The married individual entrepreneur incurs liability on obligations connected with the business activity by all his/her private property and his/her share in couple's joint ownership that would belong to him/her in case of division of marital property.

There are certain legal demands concerning business activity of individual entrepreneurs. Thus, the latter are obliged to:

(i)   obtain the license for performing certain types of business activity;
(ii)   inform state registration authorities about a change of address indicated in the registration documents, object of activity, other essential terms of his/her business activity subject to specification in the registration documents;
(iii) comply with rights and lawful interests of consumers, secure proper quality of products (works, services) manufactured by him/her, observe the rules of mandatory product certification;
(iv)   not to allow unfair competition, other violations of antimonopoly and competition legislation;
(v)   keep records of the results of business activity in compliance with legislative requirements;
(vi)   provide tax authorities with income statements and other required documents for charging taxes and other obligatory payments in time;
(vii) pay taxes and other obligatory payments in keeping with the procedure and in amounts established by the law.

An individual entrepreneur is liable for his/her obligations with all his/her property except property which cannot be imposed withdrawal by the law. The individual entrepreneur may bear property and other law-established liability for the damage and losses caused by him/her.

Besides, if an individual entrepreneur is incapable to meet creditors requirements connected with the business activity he/she may be declared a **bankrupt**[10].

Foreigners and stateless persons while performing business activity must have the same rights and the same obligations as citizens of Ukraine, unless other rules are provided by the Economic Code and other laws[11].

---

[9] The Civil Code of Ukraine, Article 34
[10] The Civil Code of Ukraine, Article 53
[11] The Economic Code of Ukraine, Article 129

The legal acts, which regulate the economic activity of legal entities, are applied to the business activity of natural persons unless the other regulative rules are not provided by the laws or arise from the substance of relations.

II. Economic organizations

Economic organizations are the most widespread type of business entities in Ukraine.

By the Economic Code **economic organizations** are legal entities, established in accordance with the Civil Code, state, municipal and other enterprises set up upon the provisions of the Economic Code, as well as other legal entities that conduct economic activity, and are registered in keeping with the procedure established by the law[12].

1. Legal entity

A **legal entity** is an organization, an artificial legal being, established and incorporated according to the procedure specified by the law. Legal entity as a person that is separate and distinct from those who create it, may enter into agreements or contracts, assume obligations, incur and pay debts, sue and be sued, and be held responsible for its actions.

A legal entity of the Private Law (hereinafter – legal entity) is organized on the basis of constituent documents which should be executed in writing and signed by all its members (founders). A legal entity can be created and act on the basis of a **model charter**[13], which after its adoption by the participants becomes a constituent document. The founders (participants) of a legal entity formed on the basis of a model charter approve the charter and carry out activities on its base.

Legal entity may be created by integration of natural persons and (or) the assets or organized by enforced segregating (separating) of the other legal entity.

Legal entity is deemed as created at the date of its state registration.

The Civil Code operates with two notions concerning a legal entity. These are **legal capacity**[14] and **legal capability**[15] of a legal entity.

---

[12] The Economic Code of Ukraine, Article 55, Part II
[13] On State Registration of Legal Entities and Individual Entrepreneurs (the Law of Ukraine), Article 1
[14] The Civil Code of Ukraine, Article 91
[15] The Civil Code of Ukraine, Article 92

A legal entity has civil rights and obligations similar to those a natural person has (**legal capacity**), and except those, which by their nature may belong only to a human. By the capacity empowered to the legal entity the latter may carry out separate kinds of activity, the list of which must be specified by the law, after receiving thereby the special approval (license). The legal capacity may be restricted only by a court decision. It occurs from the moment of its creation and must terminate from the day of entering the record on its termination to the Unified State Register.

A legal entity is entitled to the inviolability of its business reputation, inviolability of correspondence, information and other **personal non-property rights**. Personal non-property rights of a legal entity are protected the way envisaged by the law for protection of personal non-property rights of a natural person.

A legal entity acquires civil rights and obligations and exercises them (**legal capability**) through the bodies acting in accordance with the constituent documents and the law.

Procedure for the creation of a legal entity's bodies is specified by its constituent documents and the law. In cases specified by the law, the legal entity may acquire civil rights and obligations and exercise them through its members.

The body or the person, who acts on its behalf, is obliged to perform fair and reasonable actions in the interests of the legal entity and not to exceed his/her/its powers. In relations with the third parties, the limitation of powers of the legal entity is not effective except cases when the legal entity is able to prove that the third party knew about such restrictions.

If members of a legal entity's body and other persons, who act on behalf of the legal entity, violate their obligations regarding representation, they must bear joint responsibility for the losses inflicted thereby to the legal entity.

A legal entity must have a name containing information on its legal form and on the nature of its activity. In addition to the full name, the legal entity may have an abbreviated name. If the legal entity is a business company, it may have a commercial (brand) name registered according to the procedure established by the law.

The name of the legal entity must be pointed out in its constituent documents and included to the Unified State Register.

In case of changing its name a legal entity is obliged to publish the announcement thereon in print media where the information on legal entity state registration is published and to notify thereof all persons with whom it has contractual relations.

A legal entity is not entitled to use the name of any other legal entity.

Besides the name of the legal entity the **location** of the legal entity is its constitutive feature. Thus, the legal entity's location is the actual place of business activity or the location of the office, which conducts the daily operations, management and accounting of a legal entity (the place of its management body).

The Civil Code defines cases when the activity of the legal entity is conducted not from the legal entity's location but from other places.

Legal entities may have **separated subdivisions** which perform all or a part of its functions or represents and protects the legal entity's interests[16].

A **branch** is a separated subdivision of a legal entity situated outside its location that performs all or a part of its functions.

A **representative office** is a separated subdivision of a legal entity situated outside its location that represents and protects the legal entity's interests.

Branches and representative offices are not considered legal entities. They obtain the property of the legal entity that created them, and act on the basis of the regulations approved by it.

Heads of branches and representative offices are appointed by the legal entity and act on the basis of power of attorney issued to them. Information about branches and representative offices of legal entities must be included in the Unified State Register.

Legal entity must incur the liability on its obligations with all property it owns. The participant (founder) of the legal entity is not liable for obligations of the legal entity and the legal entity must not answer for the obligations of its member (founder) except if it is established by constituent documents and the law. Persons, who create the legal entity, must incur joint liability on

---

[16] The Civil Code of Ukraine, Article 95

obligations that may occur prior to its state registration. Legal entity must be responsible for obligations of its participants (founders), which are associated with its creation, only in the case of subsequent approval of their actions by the relevant authority of the legal entity.

2. Enterprise

Upon the provisions of the Economic Code of Ukraine an **enterprise** is an independent business entity that is set up by a competent state authority or local government, or other parties for the purpose of satisfaction of public or personal needs through regular production, scientific, research, trade, and other activities in keeping with the procedure established by the legislature of Ukraine.

An enterprise acts on the provisions of its charter or model charter. Enterprises regardless forms of ownership as well as organizational and legal forms have equal rights and obligations, and may be set up both for entrepreneurship and non-profit economic activity.

An enterprise is a legal entity which has a separated property, its own balance, accounts in banking institutions, and seals. An enterprise does not incorporate other legal entities[17].

Depending on forms of ownership there are following types of enterprises in Ukraine:

1/ private enterprise that acts on the basis of private property of individuals or a business entity;

2/ collective property enterprise that acts on the basis of collective property;

3/ municipal enterprise that acts on the basis of municipal property of a territorial community;

4/ state-owned enterprise that acts on the basis of state property;

5/ enterprise set up on a mixed ownership form (on the basis of combination of property of various ownership forms);

6/ joint municipal enterprise that acts on the basis of agreement of co-financing (holding) of corresponding territorial communities, parties of cooperation[18].

---

[17] The Economic Code of Ukraine, Article 62
[18] The Economic Code of Ukraine, Article 63

Other types of enterprises envisaged by the law may also operate in Ukraine. For enterprises of certain types and organizational forms the law may establish peculiarities of conducting economic activity.

An enterprise independently determines its organizational structure, the number of employees and the personnel arrangements.

Thus, an enterprise may consist of production structural units (productions areas, workshops, departments, divisions, groups, bureaus, laboratories, etc.), as well as functional structural units of the management office (administrations, departments, bureaus, services, etc.).

Functions, rights and obligations of structural units of an enterprise must be established by special provisions, approved in keeping with the procedure, determined by the charter of an enterprise or other constituent documents.

An enterprise is entitled to set up affiliates, representatives, departments and other separate units, which do not have the legal entity status, act on the basis of a relevant provision, approved by an enterprise, and may open accounts in banking institutions.

If separated units of enterprises, located outside Ukraine, conduct business activity within the territory of Ukraine, their activity must be regulated by the Economic Code and other Ukrainian laws.

Enterprises except for state and municipal enterprises are required to establish their **ultimate beneficial owner (controller)**[19], regularly update and

---

[19] **Ultimate beneficial owner (controller)** – a physical person, which regardless of formal ownership has the ability to exercise decisive influence on the management or business activities of a legal entity directly or through other persons, in particular through the realization of the right of ownership or use of all assets or a significant part, of the right of decisive influence on the formation of the composition, voting results, as well as the transactions that give the possibility to determine the conditions of economic activity, to give binding instructions or to perform the functions of the authority management, or which has the ability to exercise influence through direct or indirect (through another physical or legal person) the possession by one person alone or together with related individuals and/or legal persons shares in the legal entity in the amount of 25 per cent or more of the authorized capital or voting rights in a legal entity. In this case the ultimate beneficial owner (controller) cannot be a person who has the formal right to 25 per cent or more of the authorized capital or voting rights in a legal entity, but is an agent, nominal holder) or is merely an intermediary with respect to such rights. (On prevention and counteraction to

store information about it and submit it to the state registrar in the cases and to the extent provided by law[20].

Enterprise management is performed according to its constituent documents based on the combination of the owner's rights as to the economic disposal of his/her/its property, and participation of the personnel in management.

The owner exercises his/her/its rights as to enterprise management directly or through authorized bodies in accordance with the enterprise charter or other constituent documents. To manage the economic activity of the enterprise the owner (owners) or the authorized body appoints (elects) an enterprise manager. In the case of employment of the enterprise manager an agreement (contract) that stipulates the term of employment, rights, obligations and liability of the manager, terms of his/her material supply, terms of his/her dismissal from office, other terms of employment as agreed upon by the parties must be signed by the owner.

The enterprise manager acts on behalf of the enterprise without any authorization. He/she represents interests of an enterprise in state authorities, local governments, and other organizations, in relationships with legal entities and individuals. The enterprise manager is eligible to form enterprise administration and resolve issues of enterprise activity within the limits and according to the procedure stipulated by the constituent documents, and may be dismissed from office ahead of time on the grounds envisaged by the agreement (contract).

All the enterprises that use employed labor must enter into a **collective agreement** between the owner or the authorized body and labor personnel or the authorized body, which regulates production, labor and social relationships of labor personnel with the enterprise administration. Requirements to the contents and the procedure of entering into collective agreements are established by the Law of Ukraine "On Collective Agreements".

Labor personnel of the enterprise includes all individuals that through their labor participate in enterprise activity on the basis of a labor agreement (contract) or other forms that regulate labor relationships between an employee and the enterprise. Powers of the personnel as to its participation

---

legalization (laundering) of proceeds from crime, terrorist financing and financing of proliferation of weapons of mass destruction, The Law of Ukraine, Article 1)
[20] The Economic Code of Ukraine, Article 64[1]

in enterprise management must be stipulated by the charter or other constituent documents in compliance with the requirements of the Economic Code, legislation on certain types of enterprises, the law on labor personnel.

Decisions on social and economic issues related to enterprise activities must be processed and made by the enterprise management bodies with participation of the personnel and its authorized bodies.

Peculiarities of management of certain types of enterprises (legal forms of enterprises) are established by the Economic Code and laws on such enterprises[21].

As it was mentioned before an enterprise is a legal entity which has a separated property. An enterprise property includes production and non-production assets, as well as other values, the cost of which must be reflected in a separate balance sheet of the enterprise, and is formed by the following sources:

(a)   monetary and material contributions of its co-founders;
(b)   proceeds, generated from sales of products, services, other types of economic activity;
(c)   securities yields;
(d)   credits from banks and other lenders;
(e)   capital investments and budget subsidies;
(f)   property, purchased from other business entities, organizations and individuals;
(g)   other sources, which are not banned by the Ukrainian legislation.

All the property that belongs to an enterprise is called an **integral property complex,** which is deemed as other objects of civil rights such as things, results of intellectual activity, etc., recognizing the opportunity of the enterprise (its property complex) to be the object of sale, mortgage, lease and other transactions. An enterprise as a property complex includes all kinds of property intended for its activities, including land plots, buildings, structures, equipment, inventory, raw materials, products, rights, claims, debts, as well as the right to the trademark or other rights and is deemed immovable property.

Exercising of property rights of an enterprise including possession and use of natural resources is performed in keeping with the procedure, established by the Economic Code and other legislative acts of Ukraine.

The enterprise may issue, sale and purchase **securities**.

---

[21] The Economic Code of Ukraine, Article 65

Depending on the way of establishment and forming of the authorized capital, enterprises are divided into **unitary** and **corporate**. Peculiarities of the legal status of unitary and corporate enterprises are established by the Economic Code and other legislative acts of Ukraine.

3 TYPES OF ENTERPRISES

The Ukrainian Law offers the large scale of enterprises diversified by forms of ownership (private, state, municipal), types of liability (full, limited), ways of authorized capital formation (by one person, jointly by several persons) and by other criteria.

I. Unitary Enterprises

A **unitary enterprise** is set up by one founder that allocates the required property, forms the authorized capital not divided into shares, approves the charter, distributes incomes, manages the enterprise directly or through the appointed manager, and forms enterprise personnel on the employment basis, resolves the issues of reorganization and liquidation of the enterprise. State-owned enterprises, municipal enterprises, and those established on the property of individuals' associations, religious organizations or private property of the founder are deemed unitary.

1. A **state-owned unitary enterprise** is set up by the competent state authority under the directive procedure on the basis of a separated part of state property, without dividing it into parts, and is under the jurisdiction of the state authority. The state authority, in whose jurisdiction such enterprise is, must be a representative of the owner and perform its functions within the limits, provided by the Economic Code and other legislative acts of Ukraine. Property of the state-owned unitary enterprise must be in state ownership, and assigned to such enterprise on the right of economic supervision or operational management. The name of a state-owned unitary enterprise must contain the words "state-owned enterprise".

A state-owned unitary enterprise is not held liable by the obligations of the owner and the state authority, in whose jurisdiction such enterprise is. The management body of a state-owned unitary enterprise (the enterprise manager), is appointed by the authority, in whose jurisdiction the enterprise is, and reports to this authority. The law may determine peculiarities of the status of the state unitary enterprise manager, including introduction of a higher liability of the manager for the results of enterprise activity. State unitary enterprises act as **state-owned commercial enterprises** and **government enterprises**[22].

1.1. A **state-owned commercial enterprise** is a business entity, which acts on the principles of entrepreneurship on the basis of the charter (model charter), and is liable for the consequences of its activity by all property which belongs to it on the right of economic supervision. The authorized capital of the state commercial enterprise is formed by the authority, in whose jurisdiction such enterprise is. The amount of the authorized capital of the state commercial enterprise is established by the authority. The authorized capital of state-owned commercial enterprise must be paid before the end of the first year from the date of state registration of such enterprise.

The state and the authority, in whose jurisdiction the state-owned commercial enterprise is not liable for its obligations, except for cases, envisaged by the Economic Code and other laws of Ukraine.

Losses incurred by the state-owned commercial enterprise in the result of execution of resolutions of state authorities or local government bodies that have been declared by a court to be unconstitutional or invalid, must be reimbursed by the said authorities voluntarily or by court order.

The state-owned unitary commercial enterprise may be transformed into a corporate enterprise (a state-owned joint-stock company), a share of state ownership in the authorized capital of which is one hundred per cent[23].

1.2. A **government enterprise** is set up in the branches of the national economy, in which:

A. It is allowed to conduct economic activity only by the state-owned enterprises.

B. The main (over fifty per cent) consumer of products (works, services) is the state.

C. Free competition of producers or consumers is impossible under the conditions of the business activity.

---

[22] The Economic Code of Ukraine, Article 73
[23] The Economic Code of Ukraine, Article 74

D. Production of socially required products (works, services) satisfied by such enterprise, which by its conditions and nature of needs commonly cannot be profitable, is prevailing (over fifty per cent).

E. Privatization of property complexes of state-owned enterprises is prohibited by the law.

A government enterprise is set up upon the resolution of the Cabinet of Ministers of Ukraine. The resolution on establishment of a government enterprise specifies the volume and character of principal activity of the enterprise, as well as the authority, in whose jurisdiction the organized enterprise will be. Reorganization and liquidation of the government enterprise is conducted by the decision of the authority, which is responsible for establishment of such an enterprise.

Property of the government enterprise is assigned to it on the right of operational management.

The authority, in whose jurisdiction the government enterprise is, approves the enterprise charter, appoints the manager, provides permission for conducting economic activity by the government enterprise, and determines types of products, works, or services.

The name of the government enterprise must contain the words "government enterprise"[24].

2. A municipal unitary enterprise is set up by the competent local government authority under the directive procedure on the basis of a separated part of municipal property, and is under the jurisdiction of the local government authority.

The local government authority is a representative of the owner – a relevant territorial community, and performs its functions within the limits, established by the Economic Code and other legislative acts of Ukraine.

Property of the municipal enterprise is in municipal ownership and is assigned to such enterprise on the right of economic supervision (municipal commercial enterprise), or on the right of operational management (municipal non-profit enterprise).

The authorized capital of the municipal unitary enterprise is formed by the authority, in whose jurisdiction such an enterprise is. The amount of the authorized capital of the municipal unitary enterprise is determined by the

---

[24] The Economic Code of Ukraine, Article 76

relevant local council.

The authorized capital of the municipal enterprise shall be paid before the end of the first year from the date of state registration of such an enterprise.

The name of the municipal unitary enterprise shall contain the words "municipal enterprise" and a reference to the local government authority, in whose jurisdiction such an enterprise is.

The municipal unitary enterprise is not held liable for obligations of the owner and the local government authority. The municipal unitary enterprise is administered by the manager, appointed by authority, in whose jurisdiction such enterprise is, and reports to such an authority.

Losses incurred by the municipal unitary enterprise in the result of execution of decisions of state authorities or local governments, shall be reimbursed by the said authorities voluntarily or by court order.

Peculiarities of economic activity of municipal unitary enterprises are determined in compliance with the requirements, established by the Economic Code of Ukraine as to activity of state-owned commercial or government enterprises[25].

3. Private Enterprises

If an enterprise acts on the basis of private ownership of one citizen of Ukraine, a foreigner, or a stateless person and his/her labor or with the use of employed labor it is a **private enterprise** that is unitary by its nature. Private enterprise is also deemed an enterprise that acts on the basis of private ownership of a business entity – a legal entity.

Private enterprises, which are set up on the private property of two or more persons are deemed corporate enterprises.

The procedure of forming and functioning of private enterprises is determined by the Economic Code and other laws of Ukraine.

4. Enterprise of the association of individuals, religious organization is deemed a unitary enterprise which is set up on the property of the association of individuals (public organization, political party) or the property of the religious organization to carry out economic activity in order to accomplish the charter tasks.

---

[25] The Economic Code of Ukraine, Article 78

The ownership right of the association of individuals is exercised by their superior charter authorities in keeping with the procedure envisaged by the charter and the constituent documents. The right of the ownership of the religious organizations is exercised by their management bodies in accordance with the law.

The founder of the enterprise of the association of individuals is deemed a relevant association of individuals that has the legal entity status, as well as the union (association) of public organizations in the event its charter provides for setting up enterprises. Political parties and legal entities set up by such parties are not eligible to form enterprises, except for mass media, enterprises selling public and political literature, other propagandistic and agitation materials, products with own symbols, arranging exhibits, lectures, festivals and other social and political events.

Religious organizations have the right to set up publishing, printing, production, construction and renovation, agricultural and other enterprises, required for securing activities of such organizations.

Enterprise of the association of individuals, religious organization acts on the basis of the charter and is deemed a legal entity, carrying out its activity based on the right of operational management or economic supervision[26].

II. Corporate Enterprises

A **corporate enterprise** commonly is set up by two or more co-founders upon their joint decision (agreement), and acts on the basis of combination of property and/or entrepreneurial or labor activity of co-founders (participants), their joint management on the basis of corporate rights, including management through the bodies they establish, participation of co-founders (participants) in the distribution of incomes and risks of the enterprise.

Besides companies, corporate enterprises comprise cooperatives, and other enterprises, including private enterprises that are set up on the private property of two or more persons.

1. Companies

A **company** is an organization created by uniting persons (participants) with the right of the participation in this company, and the authorized capital which is divided into shares among its members.

---

[26] The Economic Code of Ukraine, Article112

A company's constituent documents include the charter (the model charter) approved by all its members and the foundation agreement between the members (founders).

A company except a general partnership and a limited partnership may be organized by one person who becomes its single member.

Companies are deemed enterprises, which are set up by legal entities and/or individuals by means of uniting their property and participating in business activity with the purpose of generating profit. Co-founders and participants of the company may be business entities, other parties of economic relationships, as well as individuals that are not business entities. Restrictions as to the establishment and participation in companies of business entities or other persons are established by the Economic Code and other laws of Ukraine.

Companies are legal entities. Business entities that became founders or participants of a company must retain the legal entity status. Companies may conduct any business activity unless other rules are provided by the law.

A company is an owner of:

1/ the property transferred thereto into possession by the company members as a contribution to the authorized capital;

2/ the products manufactured by the company as a result of its economic activity;

3/ the received incomes;

4/ other property acquired on the basis not prohibited by the law.

Money, securities and other things or property as well as other alienable rights that have pecuniary value may become a contribution to the authorized capital of the company.

The contribution of a company member must be evaluated upon the agreement of the company members and in cases established by the law must be subject to the independent expert examination.

Company members are entitled to:

1) participate in the partnership management pursuant to the procedure specified in the constituent documents;

2) take part in the distribution of the partnership's profit and receive

its part (dividends);

3) withdraw from the partnership according to the established procedure;

4) alienate the shares of the company's authorized capital and securities;

5) obtain information on the company's activity.

A company members may also have other rights specified by the constituent documents and the law.

A company members also have certain obligations. Thus, a company members are obliged to:

1) follow the partnership's constituent document and execute resolutions of the general meeting;

2) fulfill their obligations to the partnership including those connected with the property participation as well as to make contributions (pay for the shares) in the amount and according to the procedure and by means provided by the constituent document;

3) not to disclose a commercial secrecy and confidential information on the partnership activity.

A company members may also have other obligations specified by the constituent documents and the law.

Companies are divided into entrepreneurial and non-entrepreneurial[27].

Companies, which carry out the business activity with the purpose of receiving profit and subsequent distribution thereof among their participants (business companies) may be created as **joint-stock companies, limited liability companies, additional liability companies, general partnerships** and **limited partnerships**[28].

1.1. A **joint-stock company** – a business association that has an authorized capital, divided into a certain number of shares of the same nominal value, and is held liable for its obligations with all its property.

Shareholders are not liable for the company's obligations and bear the

---

[27] The Civil Code of Ukraine, Article 83
[28] The Civil Code of Ukraine, Article 84

risk of losses related to the company's operation within the value limits of the shares owned by them. In the cases provided by the charter, the shareholders who have not fully paid their shares must be liable for the company's obligations within the limits of the unpaid shares' value owned by them.

The name of a joint-stock company contains its name and an indication that the company is a joint-stock company.

A joint-stock company that conducts public offering for shares is obliged to publish annually for the purpose of general notice its annual report, balance sheet, information about profits and losses, as well as other information envisaged by the law.

By the law of Ukraine "On Joint Stock Companies" there public and private joint stock companies (JSC's).

There must be no more than 100 shareholders in a private JSC. Besides, a private JSC must perform only private placement of shares.

A public JSC may perform public and private placement of shares.

1.2. A **limited liability company** – a business association that has an authorized capital, divided into shares of the amount specified by the constituent documents, and is held liable for its obligations only with its property.

Members of the company that paid their contributions in full are not liable for its obligations and bear risks of losses, associated with company's activities within their contributions.

Members of the company, who have not made their contributions in full, must incur a joint liability on its obligations within the value of not contributed share of the contribution of each its member.

A limited liability company may be established by one or a few persons.

The name of a limited liability company should include the company's name and the words "limited liability company".

1.3. An additional liability company – a business association, the authorized capital of which is divided into shares, the size of which is determined by the constituent documents.

An additional liability company is a company founded by one or several entities.

Participants of an additional liability company bear solidary secondary (subsidiary) liability for its obligations with their property in the amount established by the company's constituent documents and being equally multiple for all the participants to the value of a contribution made by each participant.

In case one of the participants is acknowledged bankrupt, his/her/its liability for the company's obligations must be divided among the other participants pro rata to their shares in the authorized capital of the company.

The name of an additional liability company must contain the name of the company, as well as the words "additional liability company".

1.4. A **general partnership** – a business association, all the members of which according to the agreement concluded among them conduct business activity on behalf of the partnership, and suffer additional joint and several liability for partnership's obligations with all their property.

A person may be a member of only one general partnership.

A member of a general partnership is not entitled to take legal actions on its behalf and in its interests or in the interests of the third parties, which are similar to those, which are the subject of the partnership activity, without approval of its other members.

In case of violation of this rule, the partnership is entitled at its option to demand from such member either the indemnification for the losses inflicted to the partnership or the transfer of all benefits resulted from these legal actions to the partnership.

4. The name of a general partnership must include the names of all its members and the words "general partnership" or the name of one or a few members with addition of the words "and the Company" as well as the words "general partnership".

1.5. A **limited partnership** – a business partnership, where one or more owners conduct business activity on behalf of the partnership, and suffer additional joint and several liability for partnership's obligations with all their property, which may be seized under the law (full members), and other members participating in partnership activity, which are liable only with their contributions (contributors).

A limited partnership must include the names of all its full members, the words "limited partnership" or contain the name of at least one full member with the addition of words "and the company" as well as the words "limited partnership".

If a limited partnership's name includes the name of a contributor, such contributor must become a full member of the limited partnership.

Members of a general partnership, full members of a limited partnership may only be persons registered as individual entrepreneurs[29].

2. Cooperative Enterprises

Cooperatives as voluntarily unions of individuals with the purpose of resolving by them economic, social and everyday issues may be set up in different industries (production, consumer's, housing, etc.). Activity of different types of cooperatives is governed by the law.

2.1. A **production cooperative** is a voluntarily union of individuals that is set up on a membership basis with the purpose of common production or other economic activity, based on their personal labor participation and the combination of property contributions, participation in enterprise management, and distribution of the income between the cooperative members in accordance with their participation in its activity.

Production cooperatives may perform production, processing, storage and sales, supplies, service and any other entrepreneurial activity, not banned by the law. The production cooperative is deemed a legal entity and acts on the basis of its charter. The name of the production cooperative must contain the words "production cooperative" or "cooperative enterprise"[30].

2.2. Consumer's Cooperation in Ukraine is understood as a system of self-administration organizations of individuals (consumer's partnerships, their associations, unions), as well as enterprises and institutions of these organizations, which are deemed an independent organizational form of the cooperative activity.

The primary element of consumer's cooperation must be a consumer's partnership – a self-administration organization of individuals that associates on the basis of voluntary membership for a common economic activity for the purpose of collective organized satisfaction of their economic and social interests. Each member of a consumer's partnership must have his/her share in the partnership's property.

---

[29] The Economic Code of Ukraine, Article 80
[30] The Economic Code of Ukraine, Article 95

The consumer's partnership is a legal entity that acts on the basis of the charter.

Consumer's partnerships may voluntarily associate in unions, in other forms of associations envisaged by the law, and must have the right of free exit.

Property of consumer's cooperation consists of the property consumer's partnerships, unions (associations) and their common property, and is deemed one of the forms of collective property. Possession, use and disposal of consumer's cooperation property are conducted by its bodies in compliance with the constituent documents of partnerships, unions (associations). Objects of consumer's cooperation property may be in common property of consumer's partnerships, unions (associations). Their share in property is determined by the contract.

Consumer's partnerships, their unions (associations) may – for achievement of their charter goals – set up enterprises, institutions and other business entities in compliance with the requirements of the Economic Code of Ukraine.

Unitary or corporate enterprises set up by a consumer's partnership (partnerships) or unions (associations) of consumer's partnerships pursuant to the requirements of the Economic Code and other legislative acts of Ukraine to achieve charter goals of such partnerships, unions (associations) are deemed enterprises of consumer's cooperation[31].

III. Other Types of Enterprises

1. A farm is a form of individuals' entrepreneurship for the purpose of production, processing and selling of agricultural products.

Members of the farm may not be persons working at such farm under the labor contract (agreement).

Relationships, arising from forming and functioning of farms, are regulated by the Economic Code, as well as the law on farms, and other laws of Ukraine.

2. Enterprise with Foreign Investments[32]

An enterprise set up in compliance with the requirements of the

---

[31] The Economic Code of Ukraine, Article 111
[32] The Economic Code of Ukraine, Article116

Economic Code of Ukraine, and a share of a foreign investment in the authorized capital of which is at least ten percent, is deemed an enterprise with foreign investments. The enterprise acquires the status of an enterprise with foreign investments from the date of enrollment of foreign investments to its balance.

Foreign investments are deemed as valuables placed by foreign investors into objects of investment activity according to Ukrainian legislation with the purpose of generating profit or achieving social effect. Foreign investments may be placed in objects, investments in which are not prohibited by the laws of Ukraine. Enterprises with foreign investments are eligible to be founders of subsidiaries, set up affiliates and representative offices within and outside the territory of Ukraine in keeping with Ukrainian legislation and legislation of relevant states. The law may determine industries of economy and/or territories, where the total size of foreign investments must be determined, as well as territories, where activities of enterprises with foreign investments must be restricted or banned, based on the requirements of the national security. The legal status and the procedure of activity of enterprises with foreign investments must be determined by the Economic Code, the law on the treatment of foreign investments in Ukraine, and other legislative acts.

3. Foreign Enterprise[33]

A foreign enterprise is a unitary or corporate enterprise set up under Ukrainian legislation, which acts exclusively on the basis of property of foreigners or foreign legal entities, or operating company, fully owned by such persons. Foreign enterprises may not be established in the sectors being of strategic importance for the national security of Ukraine.

Activities of affiliates, representative offices and other separated units of enterprises set up according to legislation of other states must be performed within the territory of Ukraine in accordance with Ukrainian legislation. Terms and procedure of forming, requirements to forming and functioning of foreign enterprises must be determined by the Economic Code, the law on the treatment of foreign investments, other laws of Ukraine.

4. Associated Enterprises. Holding Company[34]

Associated enterprises (economic organizations) are understood as a group of business entities – legal entities interconnected by relations of economic and/or organizational dependency in the form of participation in the

---

[33] The Economic Code of Ukraine, Article117
[34] The Economic Code of Ukraine, Article 126

authorized capital and/or management. Dependency between associated enterprises may be **simple** and **crucial**.

A. **Simple dependency** between associated enterprises arises when one of them has the ability to block decisions of another (dependent) enterprise, if such a decision must be made by the qualified majority of votes.

B **Crucial dependency** between associated enterprises occurs if control and subordination relationships due to the dominant participation of the controlling enterprise in the authorized capital and/or the general meeting or other management bodies of the other enterprise (subsidiary), in particular if the possession of a controlling block of shares takes place. Relationships of crucial dependency may be established on condition of obtaining the consent of the relevant authorities of the Antimonopoly Committee of Ukraine.

Simple or crucial dependency is specified in the information about the state registration of the dependent enterprise (subsidiary), and published in media.

A business entity that holds a controlling block of shares of the subsidiary (subsidiaries) is a **holding company**.

Under the provisions of the Economic Code of Ukraine a holding company is a public joint-stock company, which owns, uses and disposes of a holding of corporate shares (participation units) of two or more corporate enterprises (except of shares owned by the state).

If a corporate entity (subsidiary) becomes insolvent through the fault of the controlling enterprise, and is declared bankrupt, the holding company must bear subsidiary liability for the obligations of the corporate enterprise.

A company (a limited liability company, an additional liability company or a joint-stock company) is dependent if the other (principal) company owns twenty or more per cent of the authorized capital of the limited liability company or the additional liability company or twenty or more per cent of ordinary shares of the joint-stock company.

The company that purchased or otherwise acquired twenty or more per cent of the authorized capital of the limited liability company or the additional liability company or twenty or more per cent of ordinary shares of the joint-stock company is obliged to promulgate this information according to the procedure established by the law.

4 UNIONS OF ENTERPRISES

A union of enterprises is an economic organization set up by two or more enterprises with the purpose of coordination of their production, scientific and other activity to resolve common economic and social tasks.

Unions of enterprises are set up by enterprises on a voluntary basis, or upon the decision by the bodies that have the right to establish such unions. The union of enterprises may include enterprises established under the legislation of other states, and Ukrainian enterprises may be members of unions of enterprises formed on the territory of other states. Unions of enterprises must be formed for an indefinite term or as temporary unions.

A union of enterprises[35] is as a legal entity incorporated according to the legislation of Ukraine. Depending on the procedure of forming unions of enterprises may be set up as **business unions**, or as state-owned or municipal business unions.

A **business union** is as a union of enterprises established on the initiative of enterprises regardless their type, which combined their economic activity on a voluntary basis.

A business union acts on the basis of a constituent agreement and/or a charter that is approved by its co-founders.

A state-owned (municipal) business union is understood as a union of

---

[35] The Economic Code of Ukraine, Chapter 12

enterprises formed by state-owned (municipal) enterprises upon the decision of the Cabinet of Ministers of Ukraine, or in cases established by the law, the decisions of ministries (other authorities, under whose jurisdiction the enterprises that form a union are), or upon the decision of the competent local governments.

A state-owned (municipal) business union acts on the basis of the decision on its establishment and the charter, which is approved by the authority that made a decision on setting up the union.

I. Types of Business Unions

Business unions must be formed as **associations, corporations, consortiums, concerns**, other enterprise unions established by the law.

1. Association

An **association** is as a contractual union set up with the purpose of permanent coordination of economic activity of enterprises that is united by means of centralization of one or more of the production and management functions, development of specialization and cooperation of production, the organization of common production based on the integration of financial and material resources mainly to meet economic needs of the members of the union. The association charter states the fact that it is a business union. The association is not entitled to interfere in the economic activity of enterprises – members of the association. Upon members' decision the association may be authorized to represent their interests in relationships with state authorities, other enterprises and organizations.

2. Corporation

A **corporation** is understood as a contractual union set up on the basis of the combination of production, scientific and commercial interests of enterprises associated with delegating by those certain powers of the centralized regulation of activity of each member to bodies of a corporation management.

3. Consortium

A **consortium** is deemed a temporary charter union of enterprises to achieve certain economic goal by its members (implementation of target programs, scientific-technical, construction projects, etc.). The consortium uses capitals trusted to it by its members, centralized resources, allocated for financing of a relevant program, as well as capitals, received from other sources in keeping with the procedure established by its charter. Once the goal of the consortium is achieved the consortium activity must be discontinued.

4. Concern

A **concern** is understood as a charter union of enterprises and other organizations on the basis of their financial dependency on one or a group of participants of the union with centralized functions of scientific-technical, and production development, investment, financial, foreign economic and other activities. Participants of the concern must assign to it a certain part of their powers, including the right to represent their interests in relationships with the state authorities, other enterprises and organizations. Participants of the concern may not simultaneously be participants of another concern.

II. General Provisions Regulating Business Unions

Enterprises – members of the union of enterprises retain the status of a legal entity regardless the organizational and legal form of the union.

The enterprise – member of the business union has the right to:

1/ voluntarily exit from the union on terms and in keeping with the procedure established by the constituent agreement or the charter of the union;

2/ be a member of other enterprise unions, unless other rules are provided by the law, the constituent agreement or the charter;

3/ obtain information related to enterprise interests from the union;

4/ receive a share of profit from the activity of the union of enterprises according to its charter.

The enterprise may as well have other rights envisaged by the constituent agreement or the charter of the business union.

The enterprise that is a member of a state-owned or municipal business union shall without the consent of the union neither exit, nor unite its activity with other business entities, as well as nor make decisions on its activity termination.

Decisions on forming a union of enterprises association (the constituent agreement) and the charter of the union must be approved by the Antimonopoly Committee of Ukraine.

Business unions have superior management body (general meeting) and set up executive body as envisaged by the charter of the business union.

The superior body of the business union:

(i) approves the charter of the business union, and makes changes thereto;

(ii) resolves issues on accepting new members to the union and exclusion of participants from its membership;

(iii) forms an executive body of the union according to its charter or agreement;

(iv) resolves financial and other issues in accordance with the constituent documents of the union.

The executive body of the union (collective or individual) resolves current issues, which according to the charter or agreement are within its competence.

Management of the state-owned (municipal) business union is exercised by the board of the union and the general director of the union who is appointed and dismissed from office by the body that adopted the decision on the formation of the union. The composition of the board as well as the procedure of managing of the state-owned (municipal) business union is determined by the charter of the union. Management of the current activity of the union of enterprises may be vested in the administration of one of the enterprises (the main enterprise of the union) subject to conditions stipulated by the constituent documents of the relevant union.

Disputes arising between members of the union are resolved in keeping with the procedure envisaged by the charter, or in court.

The participants of the union may place property contributions (admission, membership, target, etc.) on the terms envisaged by its constituent documents.

The property must be assigned to the union on the right of economic supervision or operational management on the basis of the constituent agreement, or the decision of setting up the union. The value of the property of the union must be reflected in its balance sheet.

The business union has the right by the decision of its superior body to establish unitary enterprises, affiliates, representative offices, as well as to be a member (founder) of companies. Enterprises that are set up by the business union act in compliance with the provisions of the Economic Code, other laws and the enterprise charter, approved by the union.

The union of enterprises is not held liable for obligations of its members, and member enterprises are not held liable for obligations of the union, unless other rules are stipulated by the constituent agreement or the charter of the union.

The enterprises – participants of the union may withdraw its membership with the preservation of mutual obligations and contracts with other entities.

The exit of the enterprise from the state-own (municipal) business union is conducted upon the decision of the body that adopted the decision on the formation of the union.

Termination of the union of enterprises takes place in the result of its conversion into another merger or liquidation.

Reorganization of the business union is carried out upon the decision of member enterprises, and reorganization of the state-owned (municipal) business union – upon the decision of the body that made a decision on the formation of the union.

Liquidation of the business association is conducted upon the decision of participating enterprises, and the elimination of the state-owned (municipal) union - upon the decision of the body which adopted the decision on the formation of the union. Liquidation of the business union is carried out in keeping with the procedure established by the Economic Code as to liquidation of enterprises. The property left after the liquidation shall be distributed between members of the union according to the charter or the agreement.

5 FORMATION AND TERMINATION OF A BUSINESS ENTITY

A business entity may be formed upon the decision of the owner (owners) of the property or a body authorized by him/her/them, and in cases specifically provided by the law, also upon the decision of other bodies, organizations and individuals through the establishment of a new business organization (merger, joining, separation, division, conversion of a functioning business entity (business entities).

Business entities may be formed by means of forced dividing (separation) of the functioning business entity upon the direction of antimonopoly authorities in accordance with the antimonopoly and competition legislation of Ukraine.

The legal entity may be terminated in the result of the transfer of all the property, rights and obligations to other legal entities – legal successors in the result of merger, joining, division, separation, conversion or in the result of liquidation by the decision, made by the founders (participants) of the legal entity or an authorized body, by a court decision or by the decision of a public authority.

I. Formation of a Business Entity

The creation of business entities is carried out pursuant to the requirements of antimonopoly and competition legislation of Ukraine.

A decision on establishment or constituent agreement and, in cases provided by the law, a charter (regulations) should be understood as constituent documents of a business entity.

A business entity can be created and act on the basis of a model charter, which after its adoption by the participants becomes a constituent document.

Constituent documents contain the name of a business entity, the purpose and object of economic activity, composition and competence of its management bodies, the procedure of decision-making, the procedure of forming property, distribution of profits, and terms of its reorganization and liquidation.

Upon a constituent agreement founders are obligated to establish a business entity, determine the procedure of joint efforts as to its establishment, terms of property transfer, the procedure of distributing profits and losses, management of business entity's activity and participation of founders in such management, the procedure of exit and entry of new founders, other conditions of activity of the business entity, as well as the procedure of its reorganization and liquidation.

State registration of legal entities and individual entrepreneurs, which is conducted in the manner prescribed by the law "On State Registration of Legal Entities and Individual Entrepreneurs", certifies the fact of creation or termination of a legal entity, the fact of acquirement or deprivation of the individual entrepreneur status, as well as any other registration actions by introducing appropriate entries to the **Unified State Register**.

State registration of legal entities and individual entrepreneurs is conducted by the state registrar at the location of a legal entity or at the place of residence of an individual entrepreneur.

In the event of armed conflict, temporary occupation, widespread violence, massive violations of human rights and emergency situations of natural or technogenic character state registration of legal entities and individual entrepreneurs may be conducted by the state registrars defined by the Ministry of justice of Ukraine outside the location of legal entity or the place of residence of individuals who have the intention to become an entrepreneur, and individual entrepreneur[36].

1. State Registration of a Legal Entity

A legal entity is established from the date of its state registration. The registration data included to state registration in the Unified State Register are

---

[36] On State Registration of Legal Entities and Individual Entrepreneurs, the Law of Ukraine, Article 5

open to public. Grounds for refusal in state registration of a legal entity are established by law. Refusal in the state registration of the legal entity on grounds other than established by law is not allowed. Refusal in the state registration, as well as a delay in its implementation may be appealed in court.

The Unified State Register includes information on legal form, name, location, management bodies, branches and representative offices of a legal entity, and other information as prescribed by law.

Changes to the constituent documents of a legal entity, which relate to information included in the Unified State Register, must enter into force for the third parties from the date of their state registration. Legal entities and their participants are not eligible to invoke the lack of state registration of such changes in relations with the third persons acting with those changes.

For state registration of a legal entity a founder (founders) or an authorized person must personally submit to the state registrar (send by posting with a list of inventory or in case of filing electronic documents submit a list, containing information on the submitted electronic documents, in the electronic form) the following documents:

(a) completed registration card for state registration of a legal entity, which can be served as an app a statement regarding the election of the legal entity of the simplified system tax and/or registration statement voluntary registration as a payer of value added tax in the form approved by the Central Executive authority ensuring the formation and implements the state tax and customs policy;
(b) duplicate of the original (copy, notarized copy) of the decision of founders or authorized body to create a legal entity in cases, envisaged by the law;
(c) two duplicates of the foundation documents (in case of submitting electronic documents – one duplicate)[37].

To the registration card for state registration legal entity, the founder (founders) or other authorized body includes:

(i) information on the ownership structure of founders - legal entities, that enables defining persons – owners of the substantial part of those legal entities and contains the following data specified natural persons: surname, name, patronymic (if available), country of citizenship, series and number of passport of the Ukrainian citizen or of a foreigner's passport, place of residence,

---

[37] On State Registration of Legal Entities and Individual Entrepreneurs, the Law of Ukraine, Article 24

registration number of the payer of taxes (if available);

(ii) information about ultimate beneficial owner (controller) (beneficial owners (controllers)) of the legal entity, including the ultimate beneficial owner (controller) (beneficial owners (controllers)) of its founder, if the founder is a legal entity, i.e.: surname, name, patronymic (if available), country of citizenship, series and number of passport of Ukrainian citizen or of a foreigner's passport, place of residence, registration number of the payer of taxes (if available)[38].

In case of a legal entity creation on the basis of the model statute, an appropriate mark with a reference to a standard statutory document must be put in the registration card for state registration of a legal entity.

In cases, envisaged by the law, except for documents, specified above, a copy of the decision of the Antimonopoly Committee of Ukraine bodies or the Cabinet of Ministers of Ukraine on granting permission for concerted actions or concentration of business entities must be additionally submitted (sent).

In the case of the state registration of a farm in addition to documents specified above a copy of the State act on the right to private property on the land of the founder or a copy of the State act on the right of permanent use of land by the founder, or a copy of the contract on the right to the use of land by the founder, in particular on the terms of lease contract must be submitted.

A document, confirming the registration of a foreign person in the country of location, particularly an extract from the commercial, banking or judicial register, must be submitted additionally to the documents, specified above, in case of state registration of a legal entity with a founder that is a foreign legal entity.

The state registrar is prohibited to require additional documents for state registration of a legal entity.

If the documents for state registration of a legal entity are submitted by the founder of a legal entity, his/her passport must be additionally shown to

---

[38] This information is not included in registration card for state registration political parties, creative unions and their territorial cells bar associations, chambers of Commerce, state bodies, local authorities and their associations.

the state registrar. If the documents for state registration of a legal entity are submitted by a person, authorized by the founder (founders) of the legal entity, a passport must be additionally shown to the state registrar, as well as a document, certifying the authorities of the person. In case of submitting electronic documents, a document, certifying the authorities of this person, must be added in electronic form.

Documents, submitted for state registration of a legal entity, must be accepted by an inventory, a copy of which is handed (sent by posting) in the day of the documents receipt to the founder or an authorized person with a mark on the date of the documents receipt.

The date of the documents receipt for state registration of a legal entity is inserted to the deed register of registration actions.

The state registrar is entitled to shelve the documents, submitted for state registration of a legal entity, if:

(a)   documents are submitted by an improper place of state registration;
(b)   documents do not meet the requirements, specified above;
(c)   the state registrar has received a court decision as for the denial of registration actions;
(d)   documents are submitted not in a full scale;
(e)   documents are submitted by a person with no proper authorities.

In the absence of grounds for shelving the documents, the state registrar checks the documents for absence of grounds for refusal in state registration of a legal entity.

The grounds for refusal in state registration of a legal entity are the following:

(i) discrepancy between the data, indicated in the registration card for state registration of a legal entity, and the data, specified in the documents, submitted for state registration of a legal entity;

(ii) inadequacy of the foundation documents to the requirements of the law;

(iii) infringement of the procedure of creating a legal entity, prescribed by the law, particularly;

(iv) availability of restrictions to fill the respective positions, prescribed by law as for the persons, indicated as the officials of the governing body of a legal entity;

(v) discrepancy between the information about the founders (participants) and the ultimate beneficial owner (controller) of the legal entity and the information concerning these persons that is reflected in the Unified State Register;

(vi) availability of restrictions as for performing legal actions by the founders (participants) of the legal entity or an authorized person;

(vii) availability in the Unified State Register of a name, identical to the name of a legal entity, contemplated to get registered;

(viii) usage in the legal entity name of the private right of full or shortened name of the public authority or local self-government body, or derivatives from these names, or a historical national name from the list, determined by the Cabinet of Ministers of Ukraine;

(ix) inadequacy of the legal entity name to the requirements of law as for the name of some types of legal entities (bank, credit union, non-governmental pension fund and so forth);

(x) prohibition, established by other laws, for usage in the legal entity name of certain terms, abbreviations, derivative terms.

Refusal in state registration of a legal entity for other reasons is not allowed[39].

In the absence of grounds for refusal in state registration of a legal entity, the state registrar introduces an identification code, and an entry to the Unified State Register on state registration of a legal entity on the basis of data from the registration card.

The date of introduction of an entry to the Unified State Register on state registration of a legal entity is considered the date of state registration of a legal entity. The term of state registration of a legal entity must not exceed three business days from the date of the documents receipt for state

---

[39] On State Registration of Legal Entities and Individual Entrepreneurs, the Law of Ukraine, Article 27

registration of a legal entity.

2. State Registration of an Individual Entrepreneur

A natural person is deemed a business entity if he/she is involved in business activity on condition of his/her state registration as an entrepreneur without the legal entity status. Information on the state registration of individual entrepreneurs must be opened. If a natural person starts his/her business activity without state registration by having concluded the appropriate agreements, he/she must not be entitled to appeal these agreements on the ground of not being an entrepreneur[40].

For state registration an individual contemplated to become an entrepreneur, and that possesses a registration number of the registration card for a taxpayer, or an authorized person (hereinafter - requestor) must personally submit (send by posting with the list of inventory or in case of electronic documents submission an inventory, containing data on the submitted electronic documents, in electronic form) or through an authorized person to the state registrar by the residency the following documents:

(a) completed registration card for state registration of individual entrepreneur, which can be served as an application to a statement regarding the choice of the simplified tax system and/or registration statement of a voluntary registration as a payer of value added tax in the form approved by the Central Executive authority ensuring the formation and implements the state tax and customs policy;

(b) copy of a document, certifying the registration in the State Register of individuals – taxpayers;
(c) notarized written consent of parents (adopters) or a custodian, or agency of guardianship and care, if the requestor is an individual, who has attained sixteen years and wants to conduct entrepreneurial activity[41].

For state registration of an individual entrepreneur, who due to his/her religious or other beliefs refused to accept the registration number of registration card for a taxpayer, officially informed the appropriate public

---

[40] The Civil Code of Ukraine, Article 50, parts II,III
[41] On State Registration of Legal Entities and Individual Entrepreneurs, the Law of Ukraine, Article 42

authorities, has a check in passport and a purpose to become an entrepreneur, a completed registration card for state registration of an individual entrepreneur must be submitted exclusively in person.

The state registrar is prohibited to require additional documents for state registration of an individual entrepreneur.

Documents, submitted for state registration of an individual entrepreneur, must be accepted according to an inventory, with a copy, handed (sent by posting) on the day of the documents receipt by the requestor with a mark of the date of the documents receipt. The date of the documents receipt on state registration of an individual entrepreneur must be inserted to the deed register of the registration actions.

The state registrar is entitled to shelve the documents, submitted for state registration of an individual entrepreneur, in the following cases:

(a)　documents are submitted by an improper place of state registration of an individual entrepreneur;
(b)　documents do not meet the requirements of the law;
(c)　documents are submitted not in a full scale.

The state registrar, in the absence of grounds for shelving the documents, submitted for state registration of an individual entrepreneur, checks these documents for absence of grounds for refusal in state registration of an individual entrepreneur.

The grounds for refusal in state registration of an individual entrepreneur must be the following:

(i) discrepancy between the data, indicated in the registration card for state registration of an individual entrepreneur, and the data, specified in the documents, submitted for state registration;

(ii) availability of restrictions for entrepreneurial activity, prescribed by the law, as for an individual, contemplated to become an entrepreneur;

(iii) availability of an entry in the Unified State Register that the requestor is an entrepreneur.

Refusal in state registration of an individual entrepreneur on other grounds must not be allowed[42].

In the absence of the grounds for refusal in state registration of an individual entrepreneur, the state registrar must introduce an entry to the Unified State Register on state registration of an individual entrepreneur on the basis of data from the registration card for state registration of an individual entrepreneur.

The date of an entry introduction to the Unified State Register on state registration of an individual entrepreneur must be considered the date of state registration of an individual entrepreneur.

State registration of an individual entrepreneur must not be later than the next business day after receipt documents for the state registration of an individual entrepreneur.

II. Termination of a Legal Entity[43]

1. Reorganization of a Legal Entity

Merger, joining, separation and conversion of a legal entity must be carried out by the decision of its members or a legal entity's body empowered by the constituent documents and in the events provided by the law – by the decision of the court or the appropriate power authorities. The law may envisage obtaining the approval from the appropriate power authorities to terminate a legal entity by merging or joining.

The creditor of the legal entity that is under termination may require termination of the pre-term fulfillment of its obligations or enforcement of the obligations.

Upon expiring the term of presenting requirements to the creditor and meeting or rejecting thereof, the commission on a legal entity termination composes the transfer act (in case of merging, joining or conversion) or the distribution balance (in case of separation), which has to include provisions on the succession of all obligations of the legal entity that is under termination to all its creditors and debtors including obligations appealed by the parties.

---

[42] On State Registration of Legal Entities and Individual Entrepreneurs, the Law of Ukraine, Article 44

[43] On State Registration of Legal Entities and Individual Entrepreneurs, the Law of Ukraine, Article 33

The transfer act and the distribution balance must be approved by the legal entity members or the body that has taken decision on the termination of the legal entity.

The copies of the transfer act and the distribution balance must be signed by the chairman and the members of the commission on a legal entity termination. These documents must be approved by the participants of the legal entity or the body that made the decision on the termination of the legal entity and transmitted to the body carrying out the state registration by the location of the state registration of the legal entity that is in the process of the termination as well as to the body carrying out the state registration by the location of the legal entity's successor.

If several legal entities become a legal entity successor and it is impossible to determine the successor for the specific obligations of the terminated legal entity, the legal entities successors must bear joint responsibility to the creditors of the terminated legal entity.

Conversion of a legal entity is a modification of its organization-legal form.

In case of conversion, all property, rights and obligations of the previous legal entity must be transferred to a new legal entity.

Separation is a transfer of a part of property, rights and obligations of a legal entity to one or a few new legal entities being created.

After the decision on the separation of participants of the legal entity or the body that made the decision to separate, the distribution balance sheet must be developed and approved.

The court that made the decision to separate, defines the participant of the legal entity or the supreme body of the legal entity (owner), who must prepare and approve the distribution balance in its decision.

The legal entity that was created as a result of separation, shall bear subsidiary liability for obligations of the legal entity from which it was separated, those, according to the distribution balance were not transferred to a legal entity, formed by the separation. Legal entity, from which the separation was made, shall bear subsidiary liability for the obligations transferred under the distribution balance to a legal entity, formed by the separation. If two or more legal entities were formed as a result of the separation, they incur subsidiary liability in conjunction with the legal entity, which was carried out separation, jointly and solidary.

If it is impossible to define person's liabilities under separate obligations which existed in the legal entity prior to the separation, the entity from which the separation was made, and legal entities established as a result of the separation must be jointly and solidary liable to the creditor on such obligations.

2. Liquidation of a Legal Entity

A legal entity is liquidated:

(a) by a decision of its members or the legal entity's body empowered therewith by the constituent documents including the expiring of the term and the achievement of the goal, for which this legal entity has been created, as well as in other cases provided by the constituent documents;

(b) by a court decision on liquidation of a legal entity via the violations made in the course of its creation, that cannot be resolved, the claim of the participant of the legal entity or the relevant public authority;

(c) by a court decision on liquidation of the legal entity in other cases specified by the law, at the suit of the respective body of the state power.

If the claim about liquidation of the legal entity was made by a public authority, this body if it has the relevant powers may be appointed a **liquidator**.

From the date the record about the decision of founders (participants) of a legal entity, court or the authorized body on liquidation of the legal entity is made in the Unified State Register of legal entities and individual entrepreneurs, the liquidation commission (liquidator) is obliged to take all necessary measures concerning the debt collection legal entity being liquidated, and in writing inform each of the debtors about termination of a legal entity. The liquidation commission (liquidator) claims about collecting of debts from the debtors of the legal entity.

The liquidation commission (liquidator) is obliged to notify the participants of the legal entity, court or authority that made the decision on the termination of a legal entity, about its participation in other legal entities

44

and/or to provide information about business entities, the subsidiaries created by it.

During carrying out of actions for liquidation of a legal entity prior to the deadline for submission of claims of creditors, the liquidation commission (liquidator) closes accounts opened in financial institutions, except for the account used for settlements with creditors in the liquidation of a legal entity.

The liquidation commission (liquidator) must take measures for inventory of property of the legal entity which terminated, as well as the property of branches and representative offices, subsidiaries and companies, as well as the property, confirming the corporate rights in other legal entities, identifies and takes action regarding the return of property that is owned by the third   parties.
In cases established by the law the liquidation commission (liquidator) provides an independent appraisal of the property of a legal entity, which is terminated.

The liquidation commission (the liquidator) takes action to close the separate subdivisions of a legal entity (branches, representative offices) and in accordance with the labour legislation provides for the dismissal of employees of a legal entity, which is terminated.

Licenses, permits and other documents, as well as seals and stamps, which must be returned to the state authorities, bodies of local government, are transferred to them by the liquidation commission (liquidator).

For inspections and determining the presence or absence of debts on payment of taxes, charges a single fee for obligatory state social insurance, insurance funds in the Pension Fund of Ukraine, social insurance funds, the liquidation commission (liquidator) timely provide to the bodies of revenue and duties and the Pension Fund of Ukraine, social insurance funds documents of a legal entity (branches, representative offices), including primary documents, registers of accounting and tax accounting.

Until the approval of the liquidation balance liquidation commission (liquidator) must prepare and submit to the bodies of revenue and duties, the Pension Fund of Ukraine and social insurance funds statements for the last reporting period.

The liquidation commission (liquidator) after the deadline for the filing of creditors' claims must prepare an interim liquidation balance sheet, including information on the composition of assets of the liquidated legal entity, the list presented by creditors and the outcome of their consideration.

The interim liquidation balance sheet is approved by the participants of a legal entity, court or authority that made the decision on liquidation of a legal entity.

Payment to creditors of the legal entity being liquidated includes taxes, fees, single fee for obligatory state social insurance and other funds that must be paid to the state or local budgets, the Pension Fund of Ukraine, social insurance funds.

The creditors' demands must be met in such order of priority:

(i) in the first turn, the demands on the indemnification of losses caused by the disability, other health injuries or the death as well as creditors' demands secured by pledge;

(ii) in the second turn, the employees' demands connected with labor relations and the author's demands regarding the payment for the use of the results of his/her intellectual and creative activity;

(iii) in the third turn, the demands on taxes and duties (mandatory payments);

(iv) in the fourth turn, all other demands.

The demands of one of the above-specified priorities must be met *pro rata* to the demands that belong to each creditor of this priority. In case of insufficiency of the entity being liquidated, funds to satisfy the claims of creditors, the liquidation Commission (liquidator) organizes the sale of the property of a legal entity. Statements for the last reporting period must be prepared and submitted to the bodies of revenue and duties, the Pension Fund of Ukraine and social insurance funds by the liquidation commission (liquidator) prior to the approval of the liquidation balance.

After completion of the settlements with creditors the liquidation commission (liquidator) must prepare a liquidation balance sheet, ensures its adoption by participants of a legal entity, court or authority that made the decision on the termination of a legal entity, and provides it to the bodies of revenue and duties.

The property of legal entity remaining after satisfaction of creditors' claims (including taxes, fees, single fee for obligatory state social insurance and other funds that must be paid to the state or local budgets, the Pension Fund of Ukraine, social insurance funds), is transmitted to the participants of the legal entity, unless other rules are stipulated by the constituent documents of the legal entity or by the law.

The documents that require storage are transferred to the relevant archives.

The liquidation commission (liquidator) provides a representation of the state registrar of the documents required by the law to carry out the state registration of the legal entity termination in the statutory period.

A legal entity is considered terminated from the date of the entry introduction to the Unified State Register on state registration of the legal entity termination.

If the assets of the legal entity are insufficient to satisfy the claims of creditors, a legal entity carries out all the necessary actions prescribed by the law "On Restoring of the Debtor's Solvency or Declaring a Debtor Bankrupt".

According to this Law the following bankruptcy court proceedings must be applied to the debtor:

1/ disposal of the debtor's property;

2/ settlement agreement;

3/ rehabilitation (restoration of solvency) of the debtor;

4/ bankrupt's liquidation.

Reorganization of the debtor or bankrupt's liquidation must be subject to the laws on protection of the economic competition.

Depending on the category of the debtor, the type of its activity and availability of commercial property, the court applies general, special or simplified procedure of bankruptcy proceedings.

The general procedure involves the application of the procedure for the disposition of property, with the further transition to the procedures of rehabilitation, liquidation or settlement agreement.

A special procedure provides involvement of additional participants, the extension of the period of restoration of solvency, the coincidence of the procedures for the disposition of property and rehabilitation.

A simplified procedure is applied during the liquidation of the bankrupt without the use of procedures for the disposition of property and rehabilitation.

The debtor, to which the judicial procedure of bankruptcy was applied, is considered a person who has no monetary obligations.

GLOSSARY

A

Additional Liability Company – a business association, the authorized capital of which is divided into shares, the size of which is determined by the constituent documents. The participants of the additional liability company bear solidary secondary (subsidiary) liability for its obligations with their property in the amount established by the company's constituent documents and being equally multiple for all the participants to the value of a contribution made by each participant.

Associated Enterprises – a group of business entities – legal entities that are interconnected by relations of economic and/or organizational dependency in the form of participation in the authorized capital and/or management.

Association – a contractual union that is set up with the purpose of permanent coordination of economic activity of enterprises that united by means of centralization of one or more of the production and management functions, development of specialization and cooperation of production, the organization of common production based on the integration of financial and material resources mainly to meet economic needs of the members of the union.

Authorized Capital (Share Capital) – the sum of the contributions of the founders and members of the company.

B

Bankruptcy – recognized by the economic court the inability of the debtor to restore its solvency through the procedures of reorganization and settlement agreement and to repay monetary claims of creditors established in the procedure defined by the law not otherwise than through the liquidation procedure.

Branch – a separated subdivision of a legal entity situated outside its location that performs all or a part of its functions

Business Entity – a party to economic relationships that carries out economic activity, exercising its economic competence (integrity of economic rights and obligations), has separate property and suffers liability by its obligations within this property, except for cases, envisaged by the law.

Business Union – a union of enterprises established on the initiative of enterprises regardless their type, which combined their economic activity on a voluntary basis.

C

Charter – a scope of the rules established by the founder (the property owner) of the organization governing its legal status, relations related to internal controls, relationships with other organizations or individuals.

Collective Agreement – an agreement between the owner or the authorized body of the enterprise and the labor personnel or the authorized body, which regulates production, labor and social relationships of the labor personnel with the enterprise administration.

Company – an organization created by uniting persons (participants) with the right to the participation in it.

Concern – a charter union of enterprises and other organizations on the basis of their financial dependency on one or a group of participants of the union with centralized functions of scientific-technical, and production development, investment, financial, foreign economic and other activities.

Consortium - a temporary charter union of enterprises that is set up to achieve by members certain economic goal (implementation of target programs, scientific-technical, construction projects, etc.).

Constituent Documents of a business entity – a decision on its establishment or a constituent agreement, and in cases, provided by the law, a charter (regulations) of a business entity.

Consumer's Cooperation – a system of self-administration organizations of individuals (consumer's partnerships, their associations, unions), as well as enterprises and institutions of these organizations, which are deemed an independent organizational form of the cooperative activity.

Conversion of a legal entity – a modification of its organization-legal form. In case of conversion, all property, rights and obligations of the previous legal entity must be transferred to a new legal entity.

Corporate Enterprise – an enterprise that is set up by two or more co-founders upon their joint decision (contract), and acts on the basis of the combination of property and/or entrepreneurial or labor activity of co-founders (participants), their joint management, on the basis of the corporate rights, including management through the bodies they establish, participation of co-founders (participants) in the distribution of its incomes and risks.

Corporation – a contractual union that is set up on the basis of the combination of production, scientific and commercial interests of enterprises associated with delegating by those of certain powers of the centralized regulation of activity of each member to bodies of corporation management.

Crucial Dependency – control and subordination relationships due to the dominant participation of the controlling enterprise in the authorized capital and/or the general meeting or other management bodies of the other enterprise (subsidiary), in particular if the possession of a controlling block of shares takes place.

D

Division – the occurrence of two or more legal entities by the division of an existing legal entity ceases to exist, and the newly created legal entities are successors in part, due to their statutory funds.

E

Economic Activity – an activity of business entities in the area of social production, aimed at manufacturing and sale of products, execution of works or providing services of value character that have price distinction.

Economic Supervision – a property right of business entity that possesses, uses and disposes of the property assigned to it by the owner (authorized body), with the restriction of legal powers with regard to certain types of property upon consent of the owner in cases envisaged by the Economic Code of Ukraine and other laws.

Economic Organizations – legal entities, which are established in accordance with the Civil Code of Ukraine, state, municipal and other enterprises that are set up upon the provisions of the Economic Code of Ukraine, as well as other legal entities that conduct economic activity, and are registered in keeping with the procedure established by the law.

Entrepreneurship – an independent, initiative, systematic, own-risk economic activity, which is carried out by business entities (entrepreneurs) with the purpose of achieving economic and social results, and generating profit.

Enterprise – an independent business entity set up by a competent state authority or local government, or other parties for the purpose of satisfaction of public or personal needs through regular production, scientific, research, trade, and other activities in keeping with the procedure established by the legislature of Ukraine.

Enterprise of the Association of Individuals, Religious Organization – a unitary enterprise that is set up on the property of the association of individuals (public organization, political party) or the property of the religious organization to carry out economic activity in order to accomplish the charter tasks.

Enterprise with Foreign Investments – an enterprise, a share of a foreign investment in the authorized capital of which is at least ten per cent.

F

Farm – a form of individuals' entrepreneurship for the purpose of production, processing and selling of agricultural products.

Fictitious Business Activity – the activity with signs of fraudulence, which gives the grounds for appeal to the court about the termination of the legal entity or the termination of activity of natural person – entrepreneur.

Foreign Enterprise - a unitary or corporate enterprise that is set up under the Ukrainian legislation, which acts exclusively on the basis of property of foreigners or foreign legal entities, or operating company, fully owned by such persons; an enterprise, a share of foreign investments in the authorized capital of which is one hundred per cent.

G

General Partnership – a business association, all members of which according to the agreement concluded among them conduct business activity on behalf of the partnership, and suffer additional joint and several liability for partnership's obligations with all their property.

Government Enterprise – an enterprise that is set up in the branches of the national economy, in which: it is allowed to conduct economic activity only by state-owned enterprises; the main (over fifty per cent) consumer of products (works, services) is the state; free competition of producers or consumers is impossible under conditions of the business activity; production of socially required products (works, services) satisfied by such enterprise, which by its conditions and nature of needs commonly cannot be profitable, is prevailing (over fifty per cent); privatization of property complexes of state-owned enterprises is prohibited by the law.

H

Holding Company – a business entity that holds a controlling block of shares of the subsidiary (subsidiaries).

I

Insolvency – incapacity of a business entity to pay monetary liabilities to its creditors after the deadline for their payment, including salaries, as well as to fulfill its commitment pertaining to payment of insurance fees for obligatory state pension insurance and other types of obligatory state social security, taxes and fees (obligatory payments) only through renewing its solvency

Integral Property Complex (of an enterprise) – an immovable property, which may be an object of purchase and sale and other agreements.

J

Joining – the joining of one or more entities to another entity. Thus, these entities cease to exist, and their rights and obligations are transferred to a legal entity to which they are joined.

Joint-Stock Company – a business association that has an authorized capital, which is divided into a certain number of shares of the same nominal value, and is held liable for its obligations with all its property.

Juridical Person (Legal Entity) - an organization that is established and incorporated according to the procedure specified by the law. Legal entity is invested with legal capacity and capability and may act as a plaintiff or a defendant in the court.

L

Labor Personnel of the enterprise – all individuals that through their labor participate in enterprise activity on the basis of a labor agreement (contract) or other forms that regulate labor relationships between an employee and the enterprise.

Large Business Entities – economic organizations – business entities of any legal form and form of property whose average number of employees during the reporting period (calendar year) exceeds 250 persons and annual income from any activity exceeds the equivalent of 50 million euros determined at the average annual exchange rate of the National Bank of Ukraine

Legal Capability – the ability of a legal person to acquire civil rights and obligations and exercise them.

Legal Capacity - the ability of a legal person to have civil rights and obligations.

Legal Entity (juridical person) - an organization that is established and registered according to the procedure specified by the law. Legal entity is invested with legal capacity and capability and may act as a plaintiff or a defendant in the court.

Legal Person – a person that has the ability to obtain, transfer and amend rights and obligations. The Law of Ukraine deals with two kinds of legal persons: natural persons (physical persons) and legal entities (juridical persons).

Limited Liability Company – a business association that has an authorized capital, which is divided into shares of the amount specified by the constituent documents, and is held liable for its obligations only with its property.

Limited Partnership – a business partnership, where one or more owners conduct business activity on the behalf of the partnership, and suffer additional joint and several liability for partnership's obligations with all their property, which may be seized under the law (full members), and other members participating in partnership activity, which are liable only with their contributions (contributors).

Location (of a business entity) - the actual place of business activity or the location of the office, which conducts the daily operations, management and accounting of a legal entity (the place of its management body).

M

Merger – an association of two or more legal entities into one new entity, these entities cease to exist and pass on their rights and responsibilities of the newly created legal entity.

Microbusiness Entities - individuals registered as natural persons – entrepreneurs and economic organizations whose average number of employees during the reporting period (calendar year) does not exceed 10 persons and annual income from any activity does not exceed the equivalent of 2 million euros determined at the average annual exchange rate of the National Bank of Ukraine

Model Charter - a typical constituent document, approved by the Cabinet of Ministers of Ukraine, which is used for the creation and operation of legal entities of the relevant legal forms, contains the statutory rules governing the legal status, rights, duties and relations associated with the creation, management and implementation of economic activity of the relevant legal entities.

Municipal Unitary Enterprise – an enterprise which is set up by the competent local government authority under the directive procedure on the basis of a separated part of the municipal property, and is under the jurisdiction of the local government authority.

N

Natural Person – Entrepreneur (Individual Entrepreneur) – a citizen of Ukraine, foreigner or stateless person that conducts business activity and is registered as an entrepreneur. A person with full legal capability, who has the right to provide business activity that is not prohibited by the law.

Non-Profit Economic Activity – economic activity that is carried out without the purpose of generating profit

O

Operational management - a property right of a business entity that possesses, uses and disposes of the property assigned to a relevant owner (authorized body) to exercise non-profit economic activity within the limits provided by the Economic Code of Ukraine and other laws, as well as by the property owner (authorized body).

P

Partnership – an arrangement, in which parties, known as **partners**, agree to cooperate to advance their mutual interests.

Personal Non-Property Rights – rights to business standing immunity, a secrecy of correspondence, information etc.

Private Enterprise – an enterprise that acts on the basis of private ownership of one or more citizens of Ukraine, foreigners, stateless persons and his/her/their labor or with the use of employed labor.

Production Cooperative – a voluntarily union of individuals set up on a membership basis with the purpose of common production or other economic activity, based on their personal labor participation and the combination of property contributions, participation in enterprise management, and distribution of the income between the cooperative members in accordance with their participation in its activity.

R

Representative Office – a separated subdivision of a legal entity situated outside its location that represents and protects the legal entity's interests.

S

Separated Subdivision - a subdivision of a legal entity which is situated outside its location and performs all or a part of its functions or represents and protects its interests.

Separation – a transfer of a part of property, rights and obligations of a legal entity to one or a few new legal entities being created.

Simple Dependency – relationships between associated enterprises due to the ability of one of them to block decisions of another (dependent) enterprise by the qualified majority of votes.

Small Business Entities – individuals registered as natural persons – entrepreneurs and economic organizations whose average number of employees during the reporting period (calendar year) does not exceed 50 persons and annual income from any activity does not exceed the equivalent of 10 million euros determined at the average annual exchange rate of the National Bank of Ukraine.

State-Owned Commercial Enterprise – an enterprise, which acts on the principles of entrepreneurship on the basis of the charter (model charter), and is liable for the consequences of its activity by all property which belongs to it on the right of economic supervision.

State-Owned Unitary Enterprise – an enterprise which is set up by the competent state authority under the directive procedure on the basis of a separated part of state property, without dividing it into parts, as a rule, and is under the jurisdiction of the state authority.

State Registration – a certification of the fact of creation or termination of a legal entity, the fact of acquirement or deprivation of the individual entrepreneur status, as well as any other registration actions, envisaged by the law, by introducing appropriate entries to the Unified State Register.

U

Ultimate Beneficial Owner (Controller) – a natural person, which regardless of formal ownership has the ability to exercise decisive influence on the management or business activities of a legal entity directly or through other persons, in particular through the realization of the right of ownership or use of all assets or a significant part, of the right of decisive influence on the formation of the composition, voting results, as well as the transactions that give the possibility to determine the conditions of economic activity, to give binding instructions or to perform the functions of the authority management, or which has the ability to exercise influence through direct or indirect (through another natural or legal person) the possession by one person alone or together with related individuals and/or legal persons shares in the legal entity in the amount of 25 per cent or more of the authorized capital or voting rights in a legal entity. In this case the ultimate beneficial owner (controller) cannot be a person who has the formal right to 25 per cent or more of the authorized capital or voting rights in a legal entity, but is an agent, nominal holder) or is merely an intermediary with respect to such rights.

Unified State Register – computer-aided system of collection, storage, protection, registration and supplying information on legal entities and individual entrepreneurs.

Union of Enterprises – an economic organization set up by two or more enterprises with the purpose of coordination of their production, scientific and other activity to resolve common economic and social tasks.

Unitary Enterprise – an enterprise, which is set up by one founder that allocates the required property, forms the authorized capital that is not divided into shares, approves the charter, distributes incomes, manages the enterprise directly or through the appointed manager, and forms enterprise personnel on the employment basis, resolves its issues of reorganization and liquidation.

ABOUT THE AUTHOR

Alla Dombrovska, PhD in Law, is the author of "Legal Regulation of the Appraisal Activity", in which the theoretical basis of the appraisals conducting is provided. Propositions for the further modernization of business legal regulation in the sphere of the asset appraisal practice are outlined.

www.ingramcontent.com/pod-product-compliance
Lightning Source LLC
Chambersburg PA
CBHW072309200526
45168CB00014B/1168